FROM
THE
HEART
OF
GOD

Brahma Kumaris

From The Heart of God

Brahma Kumaris

ISBN 1-886872-25-2
First Edition March 2003
Second Edition August 2006

Published by Brahma Kumaris Information Services Ltd., in association
with Brahma Kumaris World Spiritual University (UK) Registered
Charity No. 269971.
Global Co-operation House, 65 Pound Lane, London NW10 2HH, UK

Designed by Book Design, bookdesign.com
Printed by Leighton Printing, London, UK

www. bkpublications.com
email: enquiries@bkpublications.com

www.bkwsu.org.uk

Preface

How would we know God if we met Him or Her? Would we know? Would our heart or our mind tell us? Would we believe someone else if they told us that they had met God?

There are many kinds of knowledge, most of it derivative. However, if we are given knowledge by another, do we know it in the same way as when we personally experience it? I may learn all about being a mother by reading about it or hearing someone speak of it, but can I ever really know what it means to be a mother without raising a child myself?

We may say that we know about God because we have read and heard about Him or Her. We may have prayed or called out or sung to Him or Her. We may have had a profound experience that has given us faith. Alternatively, we may have decided that God either doesn't exist or that any traditional concept of God is not for us. Whatever our opinion is, how do we know?

This book provides an introduction to God. The words within express ideas that are like a map for the mind to explore. If you receive these ideas with an open mind, allowing them to penetrate your consciousness, letting them guide you, you may discover a new, unexplored territory, where you may undergo an experience that feels familiar. You may even find yourself being awakened to a new possibility of knowing God directly. It is hoped that this book will help you to form or deepen the experience of a direct and unique relationship with God.

Personal experience, once we trust it, is the ultimate authority for each of us. We alone know in our heart what is true and meaningful for us and when the time has come for us to heed our own inner call of truth.

We hope you will enjoy these ideas – as many students of the Brahma Kumaris around the world have done over the past decades – and find them of benefit in bringing you closer to the heart of God.

Contents

COME AND MEET ME

GETTING TO KNOW ME

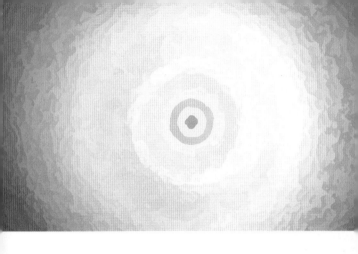

The Supreme Soul

I am a soul. I am the Supreme Soul.

This means I am the Highest of all. Even though you have given Me many names, My name is Shiva. Shiva is the one who does only good. I am the eternal Benefactor. I am the Seed, the Creator. The Creator is only One. **God is One.**

The Point of Light

I am the Supreme Soul but My form is still only that of a tiny star. It is said that I am brighter than a thousand suns. It is the energy of the eternal Soul that is so bright, giving light to the world. However, I am a minute point of energy, a soul, the Supreme Soul. I am invisible to the physical eye yet I do have a form: I am a point of light.

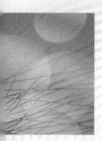

A point is small, but it is also extremely powerful. For this reason, I am also called the Ocean of All Powers, the Ocean of All Virtues, the Ocean of All Knowledge.

I am the Ocean and yet the Seed: within the Seed is the Ocean. Locked within the energy of the seed, lies the potential for all life.

I am a point of eternal light, a light that never flickers or wavers, but continues to radiate steadily. With this light, I attract all souls to come and take comfort from this light. I illuminate the soul in its hours of darkness, returning it to an understanding of divine truth.

Faster than the speed of light, I send out rays of love and peace, to heal all souls.

The Seed

A seed is so tiny, yet it contains all the elements to create. Without the seed, there would be no tree, no fruit or flowers. I am the Living Seed, and you souls are the living creation, the human world tree.

I am the eternal Father and Mother of all souls. I belong to everyone. Everyone has a right over Me. I have love for the whole world. I cooperate with everyone. I am the Seed of the Human World Tree and for this reason I have a connection with all the branches, twigs and leaves. I am the Living Being, the One who awakens fortune, the One who gives life to all souls.

The Seed has full knowledge of the tree.
I know and explain how the tree of all
humanity grows, how it is sustained and how
it eventually decays. You cannot see the seed,
but you know it is there, creating new life. I
only come when there is darkness. When the
tree of humanity is old, I make it new again.
The tree is created through Me. I, the Seed,
come in the middle of the night, and I am
hidden from all but a few. I come to benefit
all souls and to bring the light of happiness to
a world darkened by sorrow. I water the tree
with light, love and peace.

The Creator

In the hours of darkness, I come to play My role. I create a space in the intellect of each soul for silence. As I open the third eye of knowledge of all souls, I renew the energy of the soul. I am your spiritual Father and I have one pure desire for every child: each soul, each child, should become full of all spiritual treasures for many births. As the Creator, I show you how to claim a right to your full inheritance through self-transformation. I am the One who creates your fortune, who gives you new life.

By knowing the Father, the Creator, you automatically know and understand the creation. I remind you souls that your original qualities are purity and peace.

With this elevated awareness, you are transformed and, as a result, the world is transformed. A new life, a new world and a new age are created. From the moment you belong to Me, you have the right to this inheritance.

As the Creator, I am also the principal Actor in this drama of life. I play a living role in your lives and I create the opportunity for you to play your part. I give energy to the old, weakened souls to help them renew their strength. I put you back in the spotlight on the stage of peace and happiness.

The Transformer

Energy cannot be destroyed, it can only be transformed. I am the eternal Alchemist who changes the old to new, the impure to pure, the sorrowful to the happy. Only God makes hopeless souls into souls who have hope. I make possible the impossible. I destroy the old consciousness of subservience to external influences and return you to the awareness of your true qualities. It is by remembering the original self that old habits are broken. The soul's bitter bondages are dissolved by remembering Me. Through Raja Yoga, it is possible for the soul and the Supreme Soul to be reunited. Through God's knowledge, the soul becomes master of the five senses. The soul becomes conscious of itself and aware of its own original beauty.

In the laboratory of the mind and through the power of silence, the soul reaches for a new life. By becoming introspective, the soul gains new awareness of itself. Through spiritual study with the divine Teacher, self-awareness increases and the soul gradually awakens. I quench your thirst for love, self respect and self-control. When your behaviour changes, then relationships change. The search for external power is replaced by the desire to connect with the soul's own inner power in order to increase internal spiritual strength.

Your relationship with God is the foundation and the seed. As the seed grows and gains strength, the self is transformed and so, in time, the world is transformed. Negative ways of thinking and behaving automatically end where sorrow and a lack of peace are removed gently, without force. This is a guarantee from the One who transforms all that is negative into positive.

I am the One who leads you through the age of transformation. From the world of silence, and in silence, in connection with you souls who remember Me, I change everything that is dark into light. This is the period of time on earth when I destroy the old and the new emerges: this happens simultaneously – as I help the pure qualities of love, peace and happiness re-emerge, the negative qualities that bring sorrow are automatically dissolved.

I am the eternal Surgeon whose pure light painlessly removes suffering and distress. I give you the anaesthetic of pure love. You are my child and I hold your hand and watch over you as your awareness changes from the mundane to the divine.

The Purifier

I am the Purifier. I am free from physical contamination and moral pollution. I am pure eternal energy. I am a pure being bearing no imperfection. I am capable of bringing only benefit to all souls. Therefore, My part is to purify you and liberate the world from sorrow. Only I can make you pure again. The relationship of the soul and the

Supreme Soul is unique and can be experienced only at this time.
I make you pure again by tying you to Me with a thread of love. Become absorbed in this love and have love for Me, the Purifier, and all your weaknesses will be removed.

With the energy and power of pure thoughts, I come to purify the whole universe. All souls come to Me, but not everyone understands that they must become pure. Those who become pure are My helpers in releasing the world from suffering and they then inherit the world of happiness. I help you to have pure thoughts, pure words, pure actions. In your connection with Me, you are able to manifest your pure motives to change and to heal the sickness of the soul. I bathe you in pure light and cleanse you with pure love, enabling you and your heart to be free and at peace.

Know Me As I Am

By understanding Me as I truly am, you will understand everything. No one can know Me through the scriptures alone. I do not have a human form. I am not omnipresent. I am not in everyone. I am the Living Being: you can have a direct relationship with Me.

Because I am non-physical and subtle, no one
knows who I am, no one knows Me as I am.
To know Me, you must first understand that
you, too, are a soul. Your original, eternal
form is like Mine: a soul, a subtle, living
being, a point of light. A soul cannot be seen,
but it can be understood. You are souls. I am
the Supreme Soul. I come to teach you, to
purify you and to take you home.

Knowing is understanding. Understanding
brings light into knowledge. When you know
Me as I am, only beauty will emanate from
your thoughts. When you have understood
the knowledge I bring you, only jewels of
wisdom will emerge from your mouth. When
you accept My gift of pure values and
practise them, only then will your actions be
equal to Mine.

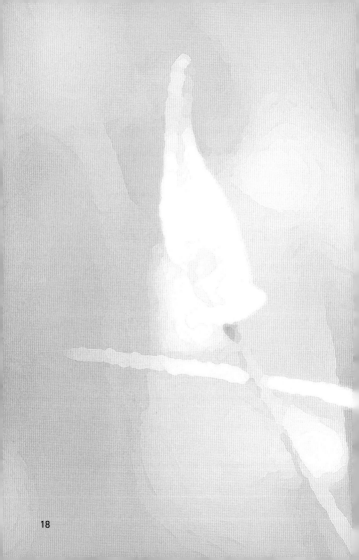

HAVING A
RELATIONSHIP
WITH ME

The Eternal Home

My home is a world of subtle light, an element of non-living matter. It is a place of golden red light beyond the consciousness of this physical world, beyond the sun, moon and stars that we are familiar with. It is the land of eternal peace, the land of silence. It is the soul world, My divine and eternal Home. In My Home, there is no gross or subtle body, no thought, word or action. In the soul world, there is no experience of pleasure or pain, nor is there any knowledge of birth or death. There is peace and peace alone.

In silence and in the stillness of the Sweet Home, all souls are in the form of the seed. Pure points of light, of energy, reside in the soul world. I am the Supreme Soul. You are also souls. The soul world is your original and eternal Home. You can travel there with your thoughts to be with Me.

In the world of peace, you are liberated from the limitations of the physical, material world. It is from this land of silence that all souls originate and it is to here that you all return. In your original Home, you experience pure peace. When you remember Me, when you bring your thoughts to Me in this world, your energy comes close to Mine, like a needle to a magnet. In this world, you sparkle brightly like a star, as the light of the soul exists in peace.

The Ocean of Love

I am the Ocean of Love; I come to show you
the path of love. My love remains unbroken
and constant. I cannot forget even one of
you. I have so much love for you and My love
is unconditional and unlimited. I am the
Beloved. You have been calling out to Me for
a long time.

I am the only one who gives you love in the form of a bestower. Because I am complete, there is nothing that I need. You need take only from Me. This is true love to make you complete. The love of the heart cannot be put into words.

I see the one desire of all souls of the world: the desire for real love. Today, no human being can give you pure and unconditional love. My children, I come to fulfil this desire – I tie you close to Me with the thread of imperishable love. I teach you how to have true love for each other again.

The Ocean of Love is made up of an unlimited amount of love. I have love for all souls, without exception. You are all My children and My love for you is altruistic.

The Eternal Parent

You are souls and I am your eternal Parent. All souls are My children. Everyone has to come back to Me. You all belong to Me. You call me 'Baba' and I call you 'Child' – there is sweetness in our relationship.

I am your unlimited Mother and Father. As My children, you souls are all brothers and sisters. As your Mother, I support you and cherish you. I have come to serve you. As your Father, I am concerned about your progress. I advise you what to do and I help develop your character. I take you by the hand and show you the light. There is always room in My heart for all of you. With My elevated thoughts, I send you signals every day in the hope that all My children will

prepare themselves to come Home. I make you into My worthy children. I love you, children. You were lost for a long time under the influence of the material world and, when you awaken, I am so happy to find you again. Children, you were not happy because you were separated from your eternal Parent.

The form of the children and the Father is the same. You are points of light. I am a point of light. I come at this unique time to adopt you and give you your spiritual inheritance of peace. I give you the knowledge that enables you to attain imperishable happiness.

Only God can say to all souls: Come, My children.

The Ocean of Power

I am the Highest, most Powerful Authority. I
am the One with all powers and all divine
qualities. By remembering Me, you receive a
lot of power and with that power you become
pure and transform yourself.

I am the Ocean of Power. I give you power
when you remember Me. When you link your
mind with Me, you receive the power to
transform old habits. By knowing Me you
leave behind distress and worry.

I am unlimited. My energy never grows less.
I rekindle the flames that have started to
dwindle and I recharge the soul's energy with
pure love and peace. The spark of
remembrance brings life to the soul.

The Inheritance

Children, I am a Bestower. I give you a divine intellect and lift the veils of illusion that have deceived you for many births. I awaken your fortune by giving you the third eye of knowledge. I change you from those who need into those who give.

I make you self-sovereigns, rulers of the senses. Through this knowledge, I make the world new again for you, My children. I create a world of unlimited happiness.

Your birthright is peace and happiness. Through Me, you become the ruler of the self and through this spiritual power over the self the world will be transformed. The world cannot be transformed by force. Victory over the self is your birthright.

All you have to do is this: Remember Me alone. It is very easy; there is nothing difficult about it. When you remember Me, you inherit everything that is Mine. Your relationship with Me is a priceless inheritance that outshines any worldly goods you may receive. I make you into My divine heirs and your eternal happiness is precious to Me. Remember Me and I will always be by your side.

The Ocean of Knowledge

I am the omniscient One, the One full of knowledge. I tell you new things. I know the secrets of all the scriptures. By knowing Me, you will know everything, too.

I am Truth. I give you the knowledge of the truth of who you are. I explain to you the beginning, the middle and the end of time. I give you the knowledge of your immortality.

I give you this nectar of knowledge to bring you back to life. I am the Ocean of Knowledge, the only One who can unveil the mysteries of life. By remembering Me, you come closer to Me. By understanding Me, you discover who you are, where you are from and you learn to understand the turning of the eternal cycle.

The Teacher

As your Teacher, I am here to answer all your questions. With eternal knowledge, I teach you to make you happy. I come to give you the knowledge of the cycle of happiness and sorrow. I teach you that you are a soul. I open the eye of your intellect and make you aware of your true nature.

I reveal to you the secrets of time. I tell you the secrets of the human tree. I relate to you the story of your immortality. I give you imperishable jewels of knowledge to make you worthy of immortality. I uplift you by making you aware that you are a soul. I teach you to have a direct relationship with Me. I teach you that all souls belong to one family, belong to one home and have one

Father. With these lessons, you change
yourself and the world changes.

The Ocean of Purity

I am the Ocean of Purity. I come to purify you, to remove your sorrow and restore happiness. Because I do not come into the cycle of birth and death, I remain pure. The power of My purity never diminishes.

I come to you when you have lost your way. You have been going in many directions and have been stumbling around looking for Truth. I come to awaken you from the deep sleep of ignorance.

I introduce Myself: I am the only altruistic server. I am the Liberator of all souls. No human being can liberate you. My ways are unique.

When you bathe in the Ocean of Purity, you forget the attachments and pain of the old world. I link you to the source of divine virtues and you experience the sweetness of having a direct relationship with God. I am your eternal Companion.

The Companion

I am your Companion, your best Friend, the One who gives you constant happiness. I am the Comforter of Hearts. Whenever you remember Me, I become present, I become your support.

In return for your one step of courage, I give you unlimited support. When you surrender your heart to Me, I promise to fulfil the responsibility of being your constant Companion. The impossible becomes possible when your hand is in the hand of the True Companion.

Because of My love for you, I remember you constantly. I decorate you with divine qualities and make you Mine. We are bound

together by the song of the heart. I, the
Supreme Soul, and you, the souls, are spiritual
companions until the end of time.

The Ocean of Peace

I am the Ocean of Peace. I live in the land of peace and My eternal, natural nature is peace. I am without desire or motive and so I can remain constantly in peace. You have been asking for peace for a long time. You ask if it is possible to have eternal peace in the world. I have great mercy and come to restore peace to the world.

I do this by reminding you that your original nature is peace. It is now time to revert to your original qualities of purity and peace. Have all relationships with Me and I will purify you and liberate you from hopelessness and sorrow.

You should always remember: I, the soul, am a being of peace. As I am eternally pure, so am I eternally peaceful.

The True Guide

The Resident of the Silent Home calls to the residents on Earth: It is now time to come Home.

I have come to purify you and take you back Home with Me. The Home of the Father and the Home of all souls is the Home of silence, the incorporeal Home where souls reside.

I will give everyone their inheritance of peace. It is My duty to show you the way Home.

Will you not come Home with Me?

COME AND
MEET ME

The Divine Pilgrimage

The Supreme Soul, who is the Ocean of Knowledge, is not visible. However, it is the One who cannot be seen who is teaching you to remember Him.

I teach you Raja Yoga – the highest of all possible unions – the unique connection between the soul and the Supreme Soul. I teach you to remember Me in order to remove your sorrow and lack of peace. When you want to remember Me, you need only move your thoughts away from the physical world and all its attractions. Having done this, you will be in a state of awareness that is only conscious of the soul and the Supreme Soul.

I say to you: Be Mine with your mind. Link your mind to My mind. As you sit, as you move, as you walk, remember Me alone. In remembering the name 'God', there isn't the sweetness of the inheritance. I am your Mother and Father. You can call Me 'Baba'. By remembering Me as Baba, your Father, there is the experience of sweetness. With this simple method, you will enjoy a divine relationship with Me. I will take you beyond the consciousness of the material world and lead you to a state of pure peace, love and happiness.

Faith in Baba and faith in yourself is the first step. Your thoughts will then walk towards My heart and My mind. Then experience the result of linking your mind with My mind. Your experience will become the proof of your relationship with Me; through this all attainments are possible.

I guarantee success to any child who comes to Me. But I know you each come close to Me according to your role and the effort you make. I never lose hope in any child. You are all My children and you all have a right to connect with Me and to be with Me. Why do you hesitate?

I only come when I am called. I do not interfere or cause you any difficulty. I am your Obedient Servant. I come to transform you and transform the world when you learn to connect your thoughts to Me.

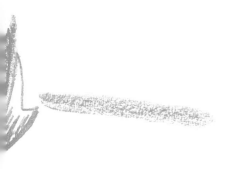

Raja Yoga Meditation

Raja Yoga means supreme union – the union of the soul with the Supreme Soul, God.

Each one of us can use our intellect to choose where to focus our attention, because we understand it is what we pay attention to that influences us. When we direct our attention to God, we are coloured by God's qualities and powers. We gradually begin to absorb God's qualities of peace and love. As a result, our mind becomes stable and free and we feel less burdened as we gain clarity of intellect. Our thoughts gain strength as we begin to use our mind in a more positive way. This transformation takes place when we link our mind with God's. The more we make this a daily practice, the more we feel and see the results. Transformation of our personality and character to a state that matches our own pure ideal is God's promise and gift to us.

Our connection and relationship with God is a golden chance to become what we want to become. It gives us the chance to shape our character and personality, offering us an easy, light and natural way of being.

You can try Raja Yoga meditation with the following exercises.

Sit comfortably in a quiet place. Allow your body to relax by taking a few deep breaths. Keep your eyes open, gently focusing on a point in the distance. There is no need to look at anything in particular.

Turn your attention inwards, concentrating on a point behind the centre of your forehead, the area of the third eye. You can still hear sounds, but there is no need to pay any attention to the outside world; just let any sounds wash over you. Similarly, you may see movement but don't let your eyes be drawn to anything.

Keep your mind focused and visualise your mind's eye as a tiny point of light. This is you, a soul. Raja Yoga meditation is not about stopping thoughts so much as creating thoughts about your true spiritual identity. Read through the guided meditation exercise below, taking one short phrase or sentence at a time. Concentrate on these ideas and thoughts and feel what they mean for you. Take as much time as you wish. If your concentration lapses at all, just gently coax your mind back to the thought and re-focus.

I am a point of light, a tiny, sparkling star.
I am the living being inside this body.
I am a soul, a subtle being of light.
I am eternal.
My original nature is one of peace.
I am peace.
I express myself through this body, yet I am not
this physical body.

I am light.
Peace is my original nature.

I can now turn my mind upwards. In my mind's eye, with my power of thought, I travel away from this place where I now sit, past the sun, moon and stars and the physical, material world that I know. My thoughts come to rest in a beautiful region filled with golden red light. This is the Soul World. This is the world of complete silence, the world of eternal peace. This is my eternal Home. Gently focus on the following thoughts:

I, the soul, experience complete stillness within.
My mind is quiet and calm.
I am aware of the pure energy of the soul.
And in this world of light, I feel at peace.
I become aware of the pure energy surrounding me.
As I experience all this, I am drawn towards a powerful Light, another bright, sparkling Star.

I identify the feeling that comes with this recognition.

It is a familiar feeling, a feeling of welcome, a personal greeting of love.

I meet my eternal Parent, my Mother, my Father, Baba.

As I come closer to Baba, I am filled with peace and comfort.

I have the experience that I can take whatever I wish from this eternal Source of Light.

I fill myself with spiritual power, love, reassurance – nothing is missing, everything I long for is available to me.

I am in the presence of the Ocean of Love, the Ocean of Purity, the Ocean of Peace.

I am close to the Living Being, the Point and the Ocean of all the attainments my heart desires.

I am embraced and enveloped by the gentle and powerful presence of One who personally knows me, accepts me and draws me close.
God only wishes to elevate me, to restore my faith in myself.
I continue to sit here in silence, absorbing the pure powers of love and peace for as long as I wish, drinking in all that I need, for as long as I want.

When I am ready, I gently take my awareness back to the physical world, returning to where I am sitting. I gradually become aware of my surroundings and, refreshed, I return to play my part in the world.

ABOUT THE
Brahma Kumaris World Spiritual University

The Brahma Kumaris World Spiritual University is an international organisation working at all levels of society for positive change. Established in 1937, the University now has over 8,000 centres in more than 90 countries. It actively participates in a wide range of educational programmes in areas such as youth, women, men, environment, peace, values, social development, education, health and human rights.

In 1996, the University's Academy for a Better World was opened in Mount Abu, India. The Academy offers individuals from all walks of life opportunities for life-long innovative learning. Residential programmes are centred on human, moral and spiritual values and principles. The University also supports the Global Hospital and Research Centre in Mount Abu, India.

Local centres around the world provide courses and lectures in meditation and positive values, supporting individuals in recognising their own inherent qualities and abilities, and making the most of their lives.

All courses and activities are offered free of charge.

Brahma Kumaris World Spiritual University

WORLD HEADQUARTERS
Po Box No 2, Mount Abu 307501, Rajasthan, India
Tel: (+91) 2974-238261 to 68 • Fax: (+91) 2974-238952 / 238883
E-mail: bkabu@bkindia.com • Website: www.brahmakumaris.com

INTERNATIONAL CO-ORDINATING OFFICE &
REGIONAL OFFICE FOR EUROPE AND THE MIDDLE EAST
Global Co-operation House, 65-69 Pound Lane, London NW10 2HH, UK
Tel: (+44) 208 727 3350 • Fax: (+44) 208 727 3351
E-mail: london@bkwsu.org • Website: www.bkwsu.org.uk

REGIONAL OFFICES

AFRICA
Brahma Kumaris, Raja Yoga Centre, Global Museum, Maua Close,
Westlands, PO Box 123 - 00606, Nairobi
Tel: (+254) 20 374 3572 / 374 1239 • Fax: (+254) 20 374 3885
E-mail: nairobi@bkwsu.org

AUSTRALIA AND SOUTH EAST ASIA
78 Alt Street, Ashfield, Sydney, NSW 2131, Australia
Tel: (+61) 2 9716 7066 • Fax: (+61) 2 9716 7795
E-mail: ashfield@au.bkwsu.org • Website: www.brahmakumaris.com.au

THE AMERICAS AND THE CARIBBEAN
Global Harmony House, 46 S. Middle Neck Road, Great Neck,
NY 11021, USA
Tel: (+1) 516 773 0971 • Fax: (+1) 516 773 0976
E-mail: newyork@bkwsu.org • Website: www.ghhny.com

RUSSIA, CIS AND THE BALTIC COUNTRIES
2 Gospitalnaya Ploschad, build. 1, Moscow - 111020, Russia
Tel: (+7) 495 263 02 47 • Fax: (+7) 495 261 32 24
E-mail: moscow@bkwsu.org • Website: www.brahmakumarisru.com

Brahma Kumaris Publications
Website: www.bkpublications.com
Email: enquiries@bkpublications.com

BKIS

Brahma Kumaris Information services ltd.

http://www.bkpublications.com
email: enquiries@bkpublications.com